BETWEEN MUSIC LESSONS

First published in 2003 by
Zelia Ltd.
Po Box 437
Edgware
HA8 8ZT

ISBN 0–9544675-1-5

A CIP catalogue record for this book is available from
the British Library

Typeset in 14/16pt Baskerville semi bold by
Cambrian Typesetters, Frimley, Surrey
Printed in Great Britain by Halstan, Amersham, Bucks.

RIKI GERARDY

Between Music Lessons

How to practise

Zelia
2003

Contents

Introduction   6

Practice   8
Posture   10
Scales   12
Detail   14
Planning   16
Attention   18

Interval—Virtuosi   20

Phrasing   22
Phrases   24
Scoring   26
Markings   28

Crossword quiz: Composers   30

Rhythm   32
Pulse   34
Harmony   36
Dynamics   38
Note lengths   40

Interval—Travellers' tales   42

Perspective   44
Control   46
Technique   48
Intonation   50
Tone   52
Expression   54
Rubato   56

Crossword quiz: instruments   58

Awareness   60
Ensemble   62
Response   64
Depth   66
Recording   68
Performing   70

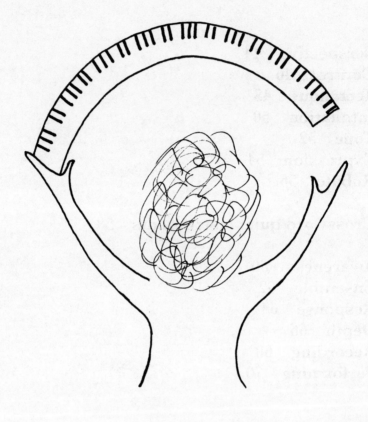

This pianist is thinking 'Now I can play it!'—having just mastered a difficult piece.

INTRODUCTION

So, it's time to practise and, after playing
through the piece . . .

comes the thought . . .

What now?

That's just what this book is about.

There may be a triangle player at the back of a large orchestra, in the percussion section. Not having many notes to play, he may also be given other percussion instruments to keep him busy.

PRACTICE

This triangle player has only one note to play, but he is thinking about it.

Thinking is what makes practising interesting, rather than something you just do (or don't).

How we practise is more important than how long we practise. This is because there is a lot to discover about the music we play.

When people play really well, you may wonder—How on earth do they do it?

Learning to play well is a journey of discovery. Each section here gives something to think about—see if it helps your playing.

In 1890, 13-year-old Pablo Casals discovered a copy of Bach's Six Suites for Solo Cello, in a secondhand music shop in Barcelona. He had never heard of them—other cellists thought of them just as studies. He thought about and practised them every day for twelve years. Their first performance created a sensation.

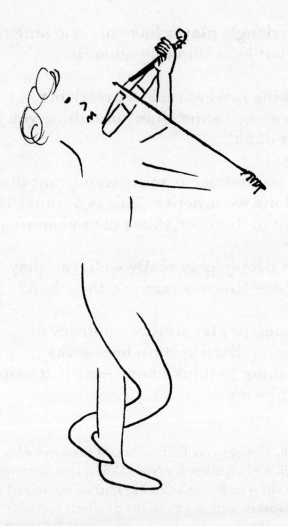

There are more violins in an orchestra than any other instrument. Try counting them, but don't mix them up with the violas, which are only slightly bigger.

POSTURE

Try bringing the instrument to you, rather than wrapping yourself around it. Find a comfortable way to sit or stand—not like the violinist in the picture, who is holding his breath in a difficult passage.

So, if playing a stringed instrument or the piano . . . it is very important to breathe. It is easy to hold the breath without realising it. Here windplayers and singers have an advantage—they have to breathe.

Good balance involves the whole body. Feel free to move in any direction, but remember to move back again; after looking down, come up again—don't take up residence down there. (Think of this when trying to get right one of those difficult passages.)

Between the stiff, held posture of a soldier on parade and the droop of a couch potato, is a point of balance—that's where you want to be.

This flute player's ears grow larger when she
practises, because she listens so carefully. When
she stops playing, they go back to normal size.
Look for the flutes in the middle of the orchestra,
behind the strings. Check the size of their ears.

SCALES

Scales are a bit like spinach—not a favourite, but very healthy. If someone can play very fast and brilliantly, the chances are that they eat lots of it.

Studies are like a jog round the park for fitness.

Even those funny finger exercises help for the rapid twiddly bits in pieces.

No need to spend a long time at the technical stuff. It is best to stop before becoming tired of it. Then you can enjoy (?)a session every day.

The secret of the great musicians is always to listen to what is played. Imagine that you are listening from the other side of the room.

The bassoon is eight feet long, so its tube is folded
in half to stop it going through the ceiling. The
bassoons sit on the second row of the woodwind.
This one is hitting the target well as he practises
slowly.

14

DETAIL

Slow practise is boring—or at least it appears to be until, suddenly, it is fascinating because . . . it works!

To play well—use it as a secret formula for mastering the difficult bits. Can you make it work with that awkward passage in your piece?

To play really well, try checking difficult rhythms and tuning at a slow speed. In this way, everything is prepared more carefully.

If you can play that fast passage slowly and accurately—then it isn't so hard gradually to increase the speed.

A couple of student pianists, anxious to learn the secrets of Vladimir Horowitz's technique, secretly spied on his practice. All they heard were single notes, clearly played, with a gap between each. They went away, completely confused. They did not understand that this was one of the ways that he worked to acquire that legendary technical control.

The cello, like the bassoon, is the deep voice of its family. Here it is well guarded as the player takes time out with the score. When the orchestra stands up for the National Anthem, cellists have to remain seated—notwithstanding.

PLANNING

Now is the time to put down the instrument—no, don't switch on the television—sit down with the score of the piece.

Having the score without the instrument, the imagination has no limits. See how the different lines of music fit together—how would it sound in an ideal performance?

The best part is yet to come. It is playing the piece as you have planned it. This is not so easy at first, as the fingers may want to play it their way—don't let them. Let your imagination be the director.

There is a special prize up for grabs—it is good musical understanding. Only those who regularly sit down for a few minutes with their score can compete.

The trumpet is like the violin of the brass family. It has a brilliant sound and is sometimes played very fast, especially in jazz bands, where speed records have been broken. Here the trumpeter is making a passage sound even. Look for them near the back of the orchestra.

ATTENTION

It is more important to practise with full attention than to practise for long periods.

Even if there are only a few minutes to practise one day, something new can be learnt.

Working with keen attention is like being an explorer.

Try going straight to that awkward passage to put it together slowly. When working from note to note, it is easier to see where the difficulties lie.

Imagine that difficult passage in your piece served up on a piece of toast. With complete control over it, chew it slowly, until there is nothing left to give any trouble.

INTERVAL—VIRTUOSI

A virtuoso is an amazingly good instrumental player, virtuosi is the plural.

Paganini (1782–1840) had a good sense of humour. He was a famous violinist who wrote *very* difficult pieces for his instrument. He said 'Any violinist who can't play a hundred notes in a second has no hope of becoming a musician.' A good way to scare off his rivals, though he did better than this when he was the first to play in a competition—all the other contestants ran away before he finished.

He arrived in Vienna in 1812, when everybody was fascinated by an extraordinary new animal they had never seen before—the giraffe. Everything from cakes to handbags was *à la giraffe* (giraffe style): in no time that changed to *à la Paganini*.

He kept his compositions closely guarded for his own use. In London, professional copyists sat at the back of the hall, trying to write down as much of his music as they could. Seat prices were doubled for his concerts and he was the hero of the hour. Someone, who didn't like these prices, wrote this rhyme about his concerts:

Who are these folk who pay five guineas
to hear a tune of Paganini's?
Echo answers—'pack o'ninnies'!

He became famous wherever he went in
Europe. Later, he played at the wedding of
Queen Victoria and Prince Albert.

*   *   *

Franz Liszt (1811–1886) was a famous pianist
and composer who, in his early years, heard
Paganini play. He achieved equal success on
the piano and wrote brilliant pieces which
completely dazzled his audiences.

*   *   *

When Beethoven offered to write a concerto
for the well known cellist Romberg, the reply
was "Not necessary, I've already written ten
of my own." Cellists also lost a concerto by
Mendelssohn—the manuscript blew off the
back of a stage coach during delivery.

*   *   *

In the past, great performers also wrote
music—so do what you can to keep up the
tradition. Incidentally, if any stringplayer
would like a challenge—it is said that
Paganini could sustain a bow for two
minutes!

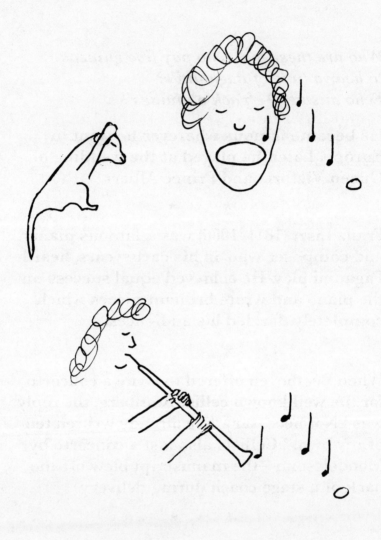

The oboe is the instrument that gives an A to tune
the orchestra. Look for two of them, next to the
flutes. The oboe can shape melodies beautifully,
but needs lots of breath control. An oboist once
invented a way of breathing in while playing.

PHRASING

Each phrase has its shape. To find it, try singing or croaking it.

Which notes are stronger? Melodies can sound different according to where the stress is put. As with words, stresses can be gentle, or occasionally more definite.

Then play the phrase, listening to see if it has the shape that was sung.

Good phrasing comes from listening and breathing—with a bit of imagination thrown in to spice things up.

This is the cellist who was studying her score. She likes to look at the whole puzzle before beginning to fit the phrases together.

PHRASES

Beginners often think of music first in notes, then in whole bars.

The next step is to think in phrases, which are like sentences. They are most often 4 bars, sometimes longer, only occasionally shorter.

Once thinking in phrases, start the jigsaw puzzle of fitting them together.

Where they fit, they may join smoothly, need a slight break or just a breath between them.

See how all the phrases fit together to form the whole picture.

Each phrase is part of a group of phrases—the pattern expands over the whole movement. For further information, try *Beyond the Music Lesson* (see back page).

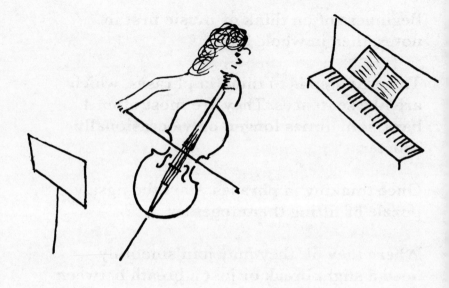

Our cellist is checking a detail on the piano score, while the pianist is putting the kettle on. At home, she keeps her own copy of the piano part.

SCORING

The piano score of an instrumental solo
has both parts included. When playing from
a separate instrumental part, only half the
picture is seen.

From the piano part, discover the bass line.
Then you can see which chords are used
and the rhythms in the inner parts.

When playing in a group, it helps to know
what the other parts are playing. It is really
helpful to look at the score before the
rehearsal.

Violinist and composer Georges Enesco had an
amazing musical memory. One day, when he was
teaching the young Yehudi Menuhin, Maurice Ravel
came by. He told Enesco that his publishers wanted
to hear his new Violin Sonata. They played it
through together and discussed a couple of
passages. After this, Enesco put the copy aside. He
then played it through again with the composer,
from memory.

The clarinets sit behind the flutes. They have a
fatter sound than the oboes. This player is
practising for the dance tonight.

MARKINGS

Written music is a set of signs and markings to show, as clearly as possible, what the composer wanted.

Before starting a piece, look at the key signature, time signature, speed indication, dynamics and any other markings.

Then think about the character of the piece, to find out how to play it. For example, *Allegro* doesn't mean fast—it means happy. So choose a speed that best suits the style of the piece.

If the music has a dance rhythm, find out about the steps of the dance.

Use all the markings as a starting point for bringing the music to life.

Develop the eye of a detective, who immediately spots clues and information. Take in all the markings with a casual glance around the score.

CROSSWORD QUIZ: COMPOSERS

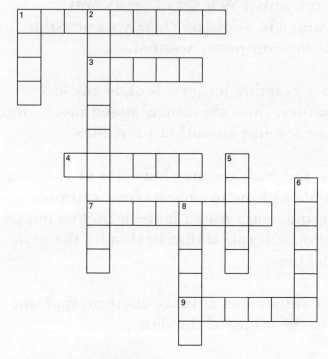

CLUES: ACROSS

1 9 Symphonies and lots more, revolutionary nature, became deaf, but still wrote great music. 1770–1827

3 Wrote 104 Symphonies, 83 String Quartets. After a 30 year job in central Europe came to London and instant fame. 1732–1809

4 Started composing and playing around the European courts as a child. Wrote 40 Symphonies, lots of concertos, great operas. Was good at billiards. 1756–1792

7 Wrote 600 songs and great chamber music. Had no home, job or money. 1797–1828

9 Wrote 10 long Symphonies, conducted the opera in Vienna. Subtract one letter from his name and it becomes the German for 'painter'. 1860–1911

DOWN

1 Had 23 children, wrote St. Matthew Passion, lots of cantatas, the 48 Preludes and Fugues. 1685–1750

2 Russian who wrote 6 Symphonies and popular concertos—very romantic music with great tunes. 1840–1893

5 Wrote great Italian operas, had a long life, gave up composing for a while. His name translated into English is 'green'. 1813–1902

6 Wrote Ring Cycle—and other great German operas (very long), both words and music. Once was political refugee. 1813–1883

8 Wrote 4 Symphonies, German Requiem, lots for piano and chamber music. Threw away 20 string quartets before publishing one. Made a recording. 1833–1897

The drum is an instrument of rhythm. Tympani are the drums most used in the orchestra. This player is in a party mood—he has just discovered a new dance rhythm.

RHYTHM

Clear and even rhythms make music come alive—that's when people want to dance.

The metronome is really useful for checking your rhythm. It can be very strange the first time through—as if the metronome can't beat in time. Then, as your rhythm improves, the metronome seems to be beating more evenly.

Sometimes rhythmic patterns can be difficult. It helps to sing or clap them, or to sing the music while clapping the beats.

The rhythm that you dance to has a regular, insistent beat. Let that energy be in your playing. Go to a dance and bring back a large sackful of rhythm.

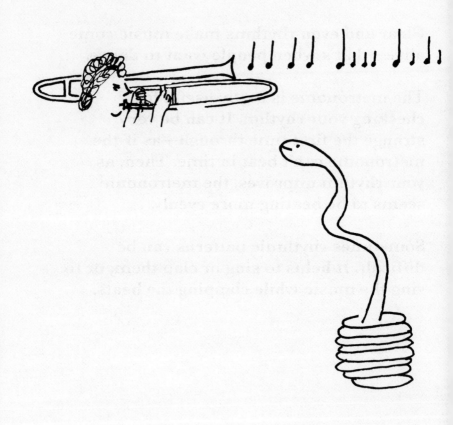

The trombone has a long slide that goes in and out.
Seated next to the trumpets, the trombones enjoy
making their presence felt. Our trombonist is
trying out the ideas on pulse. Join her if you dare!

PULSE

The beats in a bar are not equally strong—
that would be so dull.

Here is a plan for bars with four beats: try
giving more on the first beat, slightly less
on the third, and be lighter on the second
and fourth. This is only a general idea,
because the relative strength of the beats is
always changing.

It's the same when there are either three or
two beats in the bar. The first beat will be
slightly stronger than the others, but again,
the relationship will vary—try it in different
ways.

Each piece may need a slightly different
solution.

Listen to recordings of great players, just
concentrating on what they do with the pulse.
When listening for just one thing, it is surprising
how much more can be heard.

The conductor beats time to keep the orchestra
together. He shapes the music, but sometimes
talks a lot in rehearsals. It is hard to practise
conducting, so he takes every opportunity.

HARMONY

It is a good plan to think about the chords used in a piece. The movement of the harmony gives many clues about character and tempo.

The root position tonic chord is like home. We go away from home and return. As we move away, each chord has a different degree of tension. Sometimes faraway chords need to be quite strong.

Returning home may then be a relief and need a slight diminuendo—except when the music proclaims loudly its return. When people come home, they either want to rest or are bouncy and full of new ideas.

Believe it or not—there is a fun part of harmony. It is the different colours and feelings that chords give to music.

The tuba is the really deep instrument of the brass
family. In a large orchestra there may be one next
to the trombones. Our tuba player, who has been
practising very soft notes, asked if he could play
the lullaby.

DYNAMICS

Dynamics are not fixed levels of volume.
They refer to different worlds of sound.
When playing in a concert, dynamics may
need adjusting to suit the acoustics of the
hall.

For *pp* be really soft;
for *p* think of quality of tone;
mf being away from dynamic extremes,
   needs attention to tone colour;
f needs a full sound, not too loud, but with
   lots of character;
ff is very strong, but not with a hard sound.

Make plenty of contrasts. Crescendos and
diminuendos go gradually from one level to
another. At other times, changes of dynamic
are sudden and dramatic.

A large dynamic range is found through good
balance and muscular or breath control. Only the
best tuba players avoid waking the baby.

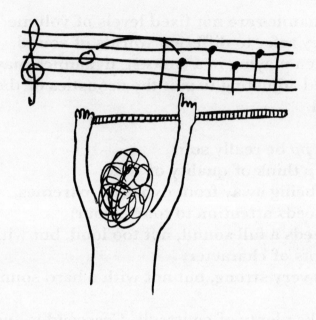

Our studious cellist is busy measuring the length of a tied note.

NOTE LENGTHS

When in doubt, try counting carefully the number of beats on each note. It's like maths—the numbers must add up. The hardest ones to get right are tied notes. It is easy to be early or late in leaving them.

Articulation refers to the way a note is played. There are special markings in the music to show this.

Some accents are biting, while others more gentle: all are followed by a diminuendo on the note.

If there is a dot over a note, it means it's shorter. A line over a note gives it a gentle stress.

Knowing the character of a piece makes it easier to decide how strongly to define the notes.

Listen to how people speak. Some people's speech is like notes with dots on; others speak in a more smooth or accented manner. The most expressive way is to have a mixture.

INTERVAL—TRAVELLERS' TALES

Violinist Fritz Kreisler had a few hours between trains at a small town in America. To amuse himself, he went into the local antique shop to ask how much the dealer would give for his violin. The man examined the instrument then took a gun from under the counter. He said he was calling the police, because this priceless Stradivari had been stolen from the great Kreisler. He would not believe that his visitor was the owner. Finally he said "Play me Schon Rosmarin"—Kreisler played it and the man put down the gun, saying "Oh, Mr. Kreisler, only you could play it like that!"

* * *

Violinist and composer Henri Vieuxtemps stopped, while on tour, in a small town. With great ceremony, he was shown to his suite in the best hotel. Once alone, he took out his violin and started to practise a rather noisy exercise he had written for playing on all four strings at once. The hotel manager burst into his room and said "Get out, you're an impostor. Vieuxtemps is the world's greatest violinist and you can't even play the thing!"

* * *

From his hotel room, composer Pietro Mascagni heard a tune from one his operas being played on a barrel organ—far too fast. He put his head out of the window and shouted "Slower, you idiot!" The next day, the organ-grinder came down the street again, with the proud sign on the side of his machine:
PUPIL OF THE GREAT MASCAGNI.

* * *

While living in Paris, composer and violinist Georges Enesco reluctantly agreed to teach the son of a friend from his country, Rumania. In spite of the boy's poor progress, the father persuaded Enesco not only to arrange a concert for his son, but also to accompany him on the piano.

On the night, no one could be found to turn the pages for Enesco, who then noticed pianist Alfred Cortot sitting in the audience. Cortot agreed to help.

The review of the concert, the next day, began: 'In an unusual violin recital last night, a great violinist played the piano, a great pianist turned the pages, and the young man who should have been turning the pages played the violin!'

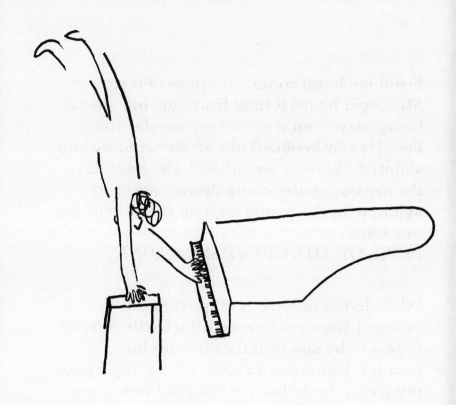

This way of practising one hand at a time has just
been invented. Our pianist is confident about his
coming concert.

44

PERSPECTIVE

Some things may come naturally, while other things may be more difficult—they need most work.

It feels good when a problem is solved and the piece no longer feels difficult.

Perspective here means seeing clearly what needs to be done. This is very important when preparing for a concert or exam.

In 1917, 16-year-old Jascha Heifetz had an enormous success in his New York debut. Two days later, he arrived at the recording studio at 8.30 a.m. He chose to begin with Paganini's Moto Perpetuo. Asked if he would prefer to start with something slower, to warm up, he declined and made a recording on the first take that is still prized by collectors.

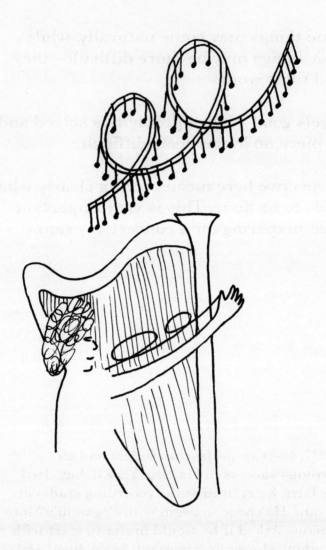

The harp is an occasional member of the
orchestra. It produces torrents of arpeggios and
sweeping gusts of sound. The harpist sits on the
left side of the orchestra, weaving spells.

CONTROL

Control is found by first understanding each movement that is made. Then it is easier to play difficult passages smoothly.

Use only the appropriate muscles. Be aware of any unnecessary movements. Control begins with good body balance.

Once there is control, it is easier to discover the real nature of technique.

Having control is like driving a powerful car—it goes fast safely but, even when going slowly, feels comfortable.

Even double bass players sometimes play fast
pieces. They have very large distances to cover. You
will know the double bass by its size—it is too big
to argue with.

TECHNIQUE

Facility is the ability to move rapidly around the instrument.

Technique is not just the playing of notes. It is the craft of shaping the notes to fit the phrase. Then, even when the notes are difficult, the phrasing can have meaning.

In a fast tempo, we need a speed at which all the notes will sound clear, controlled and expressive.

In a slow tempo, be sure that the music keeps a forward movement.

A young professional violinist came to play for Jascha Heifetz, having prepared several big concertos. Heifetz asked him to play a G major scale. After he played it, Heifetz asked him to practise it for two years and then to play it to him again.

You will see the hornplayers in the orchestra, with their round, shiny instruments, making warm, rich chords. This player is checking a note in his solo.

INTONATION

Intonation is the tuning of notes to the right pitch. It is a constant task for stringplayer— but is also part of the technique of wind and brass instruments.

The way to work at intonation is to listen carefully to each note, particularly to the intervals between notes.

When playing with piano or other instruments, listen to their chords, to check intonation.

As a group, try building up some chords— first the lowest note then, one by one, to the top note. It helps towards listening together as a group.

Work at intonation is a bit like having a shower— more noticeable when it isn't done!

This violinist is working intensely at character of sound. Let's hope that she doesn't get carried away by her imagination!

TONE

Develop a rich, full sound that really makes the instrument vibrate. Don't be satisfied with just a beautiful and even sound—look for ways to make a whole range of different tone colours.

Think of vibrato as a final colouring to the sound—something that enhances good tone production.

Keep a full sound in fast sections and in passages of short notes.

Have regular check-ups on your instrument—it needs servicing, just as a car does. This makes it easier to produce a good tone and to play fluently.

The viola is like the violin, but a bit bigger. It is good at producing rich, sad sounds, as in this demonstration. Look for the violas on the right side of the orchestra: look for viola jokes on the internet.

EXPRESSION

What are the feelings expressed in the piece
being played?

How do they change—do they become
brighter, sadder or mysterious?

There is no need actually to feel sad—just
to express sadness. After all, the next piece
might be very bright—and it wouldn't
sound so alive if you were still sad.

Violinist Fritz Kreisler toured the USA when 14, but
then studied medicine and did his army service. He
felt that an ideal day would be: to play a concert in
the morning, do an operation in the afternoon and
win a battle at midnight. Finally, he decided to
become a violinist. He shut himself up for eight
weeks in a country inn to get his technique
together. He then felt ready to begin concerts.
During those weeks, he also wrote his famous
cadenzas for the Beethoven Violin Concerto.

It is not clear if he will make it to the top of the
hill, but this violinist said he had a new way of
demonstrating rubato.

RUBATO

To be really expressive, try speeding up and slowing down a little in certain passages. This is called rubato (robbed time).

It is best used sparingly to avoid exaggerating the expression. Often, a good way is to find a balance, between moving forward and slowing down—thus keeping contact with the beat. Then it is possible to take time and give it back.

When you can do this, it is easier to handle those romantic pieces that need more freedom.

When clothes fit well, they are much more a part of you than those that just sort of fit. In the same way, when a player finds the mood and flow of a piece, it feels much more natural. Rubato is about how a piece flows.

CROSSWORD QUIZ: INSTRUMENTS

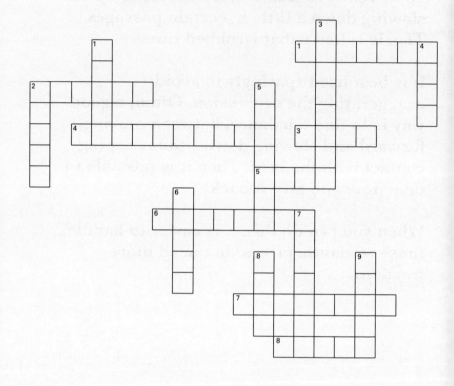

CLUES: ACROSS

1 Sets speed records
2 Lots in orchestra
3 Round brass
4 Too big to argue with
5 Double reed, needs breath control
6 Single reed, fat sound
7 Three-sided
8 Plays all the notes.

DOWN

1 Too big to put under chin
2 Attracts jokes
3 Big slide
4 Deep brass
5 Folded in half
6 Blown across a hole
7 Rhythmic instrument
8 Has lots of strings
9 Another one down.

Part of the challenge of these crosswords is that the answers are not given here. If any of these clues seem difficult, look again at the notes on instruments on the left hand pages. The clues in the first crossword all refer to composers who are very famous.

Now the triangle player has two notes to play. While he plays the first note, he is already looking at the second. A good example to follow.

AWARENESS

We need awareness of the note as it is
played:

also, awareness of what lies ahead.

When sightreading, train the eyes to keep
ahead of the note being played, but not so
far as to lose control.

Cellist Emmanuel Feuermann was given the
Studies of Popper by his teacher, who wanted to
explain some of the technical points. Before he
could begin, Feuermann proceeded to play through
the whole book at sight—immaculately.

At the age of sixteen he began teaching at the
Cologne Conservatoire. All his pupils were older
than him.

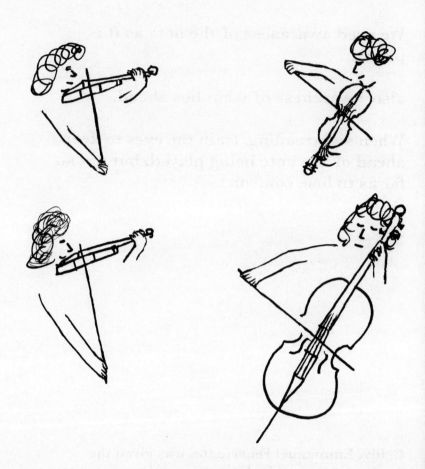

This is a string quartet: two violins, viola and
cello. They may look as if they are trying to play
together, but actually they are only warming-up.
How can we know this?—because our very musical
cellist is not looking at the others.

ENSEMBLE

Whether playing with just one other person or in a group, it is so important to play together. Not only in starting and finishing, but through the whole piece.

A conductor gives a clear upbeat before the orchestra plays. Because it is exactly in time, it tells how fast the piece will be played.

Try this by giving an upbeat with head, instrument or bow—breathing in at the same time. With a clear upbeat, all the group can start together.

When thinking of rhythm in a group, it is not just about exactness, but finding bounce—to bring it to life.

Decide together how you want to play the piece. When you are in agreement, the ensemble is always better.

In a group, remember to breathe together. To learn about ensemble, watch jet planes fly in formation.

The oboe and trumpet are playing too loudly, and the others are unhappy about it. Again the cellist has turned away, but this time it's to save her ears!

RESPONSE

When playing in a group, there is the danger that it can become a competition about who can play best or loudest.

At times you will need to be in the background: at others you will be playing a leading part.

Listen carefully to how each part fits with the others. See how the sounds blend together.

Always there are details to work at, but we also need to see the whole picture. In a group, it is all right to lose yourself in the music, as long as the attention is alive.

This is when music becomes magic.

Pianist Julius Katchen was asked, one day after breakfast, if he could play in a recording of Stravinsky's Petrushka the next morning. The orchestral piano part is very difficult and he didn't know it. He practised it for eighteen hours that day. The next morning he felt half dead, but recorded it successfully.

This is the grandfather of our long-eared flute
player. He is old and wise, and has played all the
flute pieces many times, so he makes them sound
very special.

DEPTH

To find magic in music, it helps to know a piece really well. Not just by playing it many times, but by thinking about it and discovering how it needs to be expressed.

Each time you return to it, something new can be discovered.

Trust your imagination. If you have a feeling for the whole piece, then details will work better.

Listen to other music, especially by composers whose music you play. It helps the understanding of each piece.

Pianist Artur Rubinstein had great depth in his playing. He was also fluent in eight languages. One day, he had a bad throat and went to the doctor. He was told that his throat was perfectly normal—the problem was that he talked too much.

This is our pianist listening to a recording of
his piece by a famous pianist. It is a *very* old
recording, played by the uncle of the cousin of
our fluteplayer's grandfather.

RECORDING

It helps to record pieces before a concert. Hearing a playback usually comes as a shock, especially the first time.

Does it sound different from what you hear when playing? Some things can be quickly adjusted.

If there are faults, work at them—but concentrate just on one or two aspects at a time, to avoid confusion.

Then try making another recording.

The tenor Enrico Caruso, in 1902, asked for £100 to record ten songs for the newly invented gramophone. The engineer contacted headquarters in London and was told not to go ahead since the fee was too high. He ignored this instruction, and Caruso's records were so successful that the whole future of the recording business was secure.

Occasionally the piano is used as an orchestral instrument. It is also used to accompany instrumentalists and singers. Next year, our pianist will play a solo, accompanied by the whole orchestra.

PERFORMING

Before playing in a concert or taking an exam, play the pieces first to family and friends. Then do some work on any passages that are less secure. In this way, it is possible to be well prepared for the performance.

If there is any memory lapse, make a note of the place and give it special attention.

Be calm before going on stage, or into the exam room. When something must be done, don't rush. Breathing slowly and evenly will keep you calm.

If you enjoy playing to people, they will enjoy listening, as can be seen here. Our pianist now knows that all the work was worth it!

Now read on . . .

also published by ZELIA and by the same author:

BEYOND THE MUSIC LESSON

If you have enjoyed this prequel, are you ready for the main action? This is the book that tells all—about music.

Designed for students of 16+ it has, however, been discovered by several younger players—because there is an easy way in. All the left hand pages have, instead of cartoons, an easy-to-read summary of each subject. It expands the ideas contained in this book.

Beyond the
music lesson

A guide to the
advanced study
of a musical
instrument

RIKI GERARDY

 ISBN 0-9544675-0-7